HOW TO SELL ON ETSY FOR BEGINNERS 2024

Your Complete Etsy Starter Kit

Scarlett Anderson

Table of Contents

INTRODUCTION

What is Etsy?

Etsy is an online marketplace that focuses on handmade, vintage, and unique factory-manufactured items. It provides a platform for individual sellers and small businesses to sell their handmade or vintage goods, as well as craft supplies and unique factory-made items. Founded in 2005, Etsy has grown into a global community connecting millions of buyers and sellers, fostering a marketplace where people can discover, connect, and purchase distinctive items often not found in conventional retail settings. It's known for its emphasis on creativity, craftsmanship, and the personal stories behind the products offered.

Evolution of the Etsy Marketplace.

Founding Years (2005-2008): Etsy was founded by Rob Kalin, Chris Maguire, and Haim Schoppik with a vision to create a platform for artisans to sell their handmade crafts. Initially focused on crafters, artists, and hobbyists, Etsy started gaining traction within niche communities interested in unique, handmade goods.

Expansion and Growth (2009-2013): During this period, Etsy expanded its reach and offerings. They broadened the definition of handmade to include items produced in collaboration with manufacturers, which sparked some controversy within the community. However, it also led to increased diversity in product offerings and seller types.

IPO and International Expansion (2015-2017): In 2015, Etsy went public with its IPO, signaling its status as a major player in the e-commerce industry. The company continued its global expansion, making efforts to reach international markets and provide tools for sellers worldwide. This phase saw increased investment in technology, seller tools, and mobile platforms to enhance user experience.

Policy Changes and Focus on Sustainability (2018-2020): Etsy implemented policy changes aimed at ensuring transparency in manufacturing processes and encouraging sustainable practices among sellers. They promoted eco-friendly and ethically sourced products, aligning with evolving consumer preferences for sustainability.

Pandemic Response and Growth (2020-2021): The COVID-19 pandemic led to a surge in online shopping, benefiting Etsy as a platform for unique and personalized goods. Many artisans and small businesses turned to Etsy to reach customers when physical retail was restricted. The platform saw significant growth in categories like home decor, DIY crafts, and personalized items during this time.

Continued Innovation and Diversification (2022 and beyond): Etsy continues to innovate by introducing new features, enhancing seller tools, and exploring partnerships to provide a seamless experience for both sellers and buyers. The platform also adapts to changing market demands and consumer preferences, focusing on inclusivity, sustainability, and expanding its offerings to cater to a diverse range of products.

Throughout its evolution, Etsy has remained committed to empowering independent sellers, fostering a sense of community, and promoting unique, handmade, and vintage goods while adapting to the changing landscape of e-commerce.

Why Sell on Etsy?

Selling on Etsy offers numerous benefits that cater to artisans, crafters, and small businesses. Selling on Etsy offers a blend of a supportive community, access to a specific market, and a platform that simplifies the selling process, making it an attractive option for artisans and small businesses looking to showcase their unique creations and reach a global audience.

Etsy attracts a specific audience seeking unique, handmade, and vintage items. Sellers can tap into this niche market of buyers who appreciate craftsmanship and individuality. It provides a well-established and user-friendly platform, sparing sellers from the complexities of building their own e-commerce website. This allows them to focus on creating and selling their products.

With a global presence, Etsy allows sellers to reach customers worldwide, expanding their customer base beyond local markets. Etsy fosters a supportive community where sellers can connect, share experiences, and learn from one another. The platform provides resources, forums, and educational materials to help sellers succeed.

Setting up a shop on Etsy is relatively simple and cost-effective. Sellers pay nominal fees for listing products and a small commission on sales, making it accessible for individuals and small businesses. Sellers can personalize their shops, showcase their brand, and tell the story behind their products, fostering a deeper connection with potential buyers.

Etsy offers various tools and analytics to help sellers understand their audience, optimize listings, and make informed decisions to improve sales performance. Etsy's reputation as a marketplace for handmade and unique items builds trust among buyers, making it a preferred platform for those seeking quality and authenticity.

Sellers have control over pricing, inventory, and shipping methods, allowing them to tailor their shop to suit their preferences and business needs.

Etsy continually evolves, introducing new features and adapting to market trends, ensuring sellers have access to the latest tools and opportunities to grow their businesses.

Overview of Etsy Seller Accounts

An Etsy seller account is the gateway for individuals and businesses to showcase and sell their handmade, vintage, and unique factory-manufactured items on the Etsy platform. Here's an overview of what an Etsy seller account entails:

1. Shop Setup:

Shop Name: Sellers create a unique shop name that represents their brand or products.

Shop Policies: Establishing clear policies on shipping, returns, and other important aspects.

Profile and About Section: Adding a bio, photos, and information about the seller or business to create a personal connection with buyers.

2. Listings Management:

Product Listings: Creating individual listings for each item for sale with photos, descriptions, pricing, and shipping details.

Inventory Management: Monitoring and updating inventory levels as items are sold or restocked.

3. Seller Tools:

Dashboard: Accessing a central hub that provides an overview of shop activity, orders, and performance metrics.

Seller Analytics: Utilizing data and insights to understand customer behavior, track sales trends, and optimize listings.

Promoted Listings: Managing advertising campaigns to increase visibility for specific products.

4. Communication and Sales:

Order Management: Handling orders, processing payments, and managing customer interactions.

Messaging: Communicating with customers regarding inquiries, custom orders, and resolving issues.

5. Shop Customization and Branding:

Shop Appearance: Customizing the shop's appearance with banners, logos, and branding elements to reflect the seller's identity.

Storytelling and About Section: Sharing the story behind the products or the seller's journey to create a connection with buyers.

6. Payment and Fees:

Transaction Processing: Handling payments securely through Etsy's integrated payment system.

Fees and Charges: Understanding the fees associated with listing items and transaction commissions charged by Etsy.

7. Customer Service and Feedback:

Customer Support: Providing timely and helpful responses to customer inquiries and concerns.

Feedback and Reviews: Encouraging buyers to leave reviews and managing feedback to maintain a positive reputation.

8. Growth and Marketing:

Marketing Strategies: Utilizing social media, promotions, and advertising to attract buyers to the shop.

Scaling and Diversification: Exploring opportunities to expand product lines or reach new customer segments.

CHAPTER 1

Setting Up Your Shop

Creating a Compelling Shop Name & Brand

Your shop name is the first impression buyers get of your brand. It should be memorable, reflective of your products, and easy to spell. Consider these aspects when choosing your shop name:

- Relevance: Ensure your name reflects what you sell. It can be your business name, your own name, or something catchy related to your niche.

- Unique and Memorable: Stand out from the crowd by avoiding generic names. Make it memorable so customers can easily recall and find you again.

- Consistency: Align your shop name with your brand identity. If you have a logo or specific colors associated with your brand, consider incorporating them into your shop's visual elements.

- Check Availability: Confirm the name isn't already in use on Etsy or other platforms to avoid confusion and ensure uniqueness.

Crafting an Effective Shop Profile

Your shop profile is your chance to introduce yourself to potential buyers and build trust. Here's how to craft an effective profile:

- **About Section:** Write a compelling story about your brand. Share what inspires you, your journey, and what makes your products special.

- **Photos and Visuals:** Include photos of yourself or your team, workspace, or production process to add a personal touch. This helps buyers connect with your brand.

- **Contact Information:** Provide clear and accessible contact details. This builds trust and makes it easy for buyers to reach out with questions or custom requests.

- **Shop Policies:** Clearly outline shipping, return, and exchange policies. Transparency in policies helps manage buyer expectations and reduces disputes.

Building an Appealing Product Portfolio

Your product portfolio showcases what you offer. It's crucial to make a positive impression and encourage buyers to explore further. Here's how to build an appealing portfolio:

- Diverse Offerings: Display a variety of products within your niche. Show range in colors, sizes, or styles to cater to different preferences.

- Quality Over Quantity: Start with a few high-quality listings rather than numerous mediocre ones. Quality products attract buyers and build credibility.

- Detailed Descriptions: Write clear and detailed descriptions for each product. Highlight unique features, materials used, sizing information, and care instructions.

- Consistent Branding: Maintain a consistent aesthetic across your listings. Use similar backgrounds, fonts, and photography styles to create a cohesive look.

Photography and Visuals for Listings

- Photographs are your shop's visual ambassador. They can make or break a sale. Consider the following tips for impactful visuals:

- High-Quality Images: Use high-resolution, well-lit images that clearly showcase your products. Multiple angles and close-ups help buyers visualize what they're purchasing.

- Clean Backgrounds: Use neutral or complementary backgrounds to make your product stand out. Avoid clutter that distracts from the item being sold.

- Lifestyle Shots (if applicable): Show your product in use or styled in a context that resonates with your target audience. Lifestyle images help buyers envision owning your product.

- Consistency Across Listings: Maintain a consistent style and format for all your photos. This creates a cohesive and professional look across your shop.

Step By Step Process Of Creating An Etsy Seller Accounts

1. **Visit Etsy's Website:** Go to www.etsy.com to get started.
2. **Sign Up:** At the top right corner of the homepage, click on "Sign in" or "Register" if you don't have an account.
3. **Choose Your Preferences:**
   - Language and Country: Select your preferred language and country.
   - Account Type: Opt for "Sell on Etsy" to create a seller account.
4. **Enter Shop Preferences:**
   - Shop Language: Choose the primary language for your shop.

Shop Country: Select the country where your products will be located or shipped from.

5. **Create Your Shop:**

   Shop Name: Enter a unique name for your shop. Ensure it reflects your brand and is not already in use.

   Start Listing: Click on "Open your Etsy shop" to begin setting up your shop.

6. **Add Listings:**

   Product Photos: Upload high-quality images of your products.

   Product Details: Enter details such as title, description, price, quantity, and shipping information for each item.

7. **Complete Your Shop Profile:**

   About Section: Write a compelling story about your brand and what inspires your creations.

   Shop Policies: Set clear policies for shipping, returns, and other important aspects.

8. **Payment Setup:**

   Payment Method: Choose your preferred payment method for receiving funds from sales.

   Billing Information: Provide necessary billing details for Etsy fees and charges.

9. **Review and Launch:**

   Shop Preview: Review your shop to ensure all information and listings are accurate.

   Launch Your Shop: Once satisfied, click on "Open your shop" to make it live on Etsy.

10. **Confirmation and Verification:**

- Confirmation Email: Check your email for a confirmation from Etsy regarding your new shop.
- Verify Your Account: Follow any additional steps or verification processes prompted by Etsy.

11. **Start Selling:** Once your shop is live, start promoting your listings, managing orders, and engaging with potential buyers.

Remember, creating an Etsy seller account is free, but there are fees associated with listing items and selling on the platform. Ensure you familiarize yourself with Etsy's seller policies, fees, and best practices to maximize your shop's success

CHAPTER 2

Optimizing Your Listings

By optimizing listings, crafting engaging product pages, and mastering SEO, you're positioning your Etsy shop for greater visibility, increased buyer engagement, and higher chances of sales. These strategies collectively enhance your shop's performance and impact its success within the Etsy marketplace.

Creating Compelling Visuals

Optimizing your listings is a fundamental step in attracting buyers on Etsy. Compelling visuals are the cornerstone – use high-quality images that showcase your product from various angles, emphasizing unique details and features. Titles play a pivotal role; craft concise, descriptive titles utilizing keywords relevant to your product and what potential buyers might search for. Pair these with detailed descriptions, including materials, dimensions, color options, and customization details. A strategic pricing strategy, considering value, uniqueness, and production costs, contributes to the overall appeal of your listings.

Creating Compelling Product Pages

Moving beyond mere listings to creating compelling product pages is essential. Engage your audience through storytelling, sharing the story behind your product – the inspiration, creation process, and what makes it special. Highlight the Unique Selling Proposition (USP) – what sets your product apart from others. Emphasize its benefits, quality, or any unique features that resonate with potential buyers. Adopt a customer-centric approach, addressing potential concerns proactively, and guiding buyers with clear Call-to-Action (CTA) buttons.

Mastering SEO and Keywords

Mastering SEO and keywords is key to ensuring your listings are discoverable. Conduct thorough keyword research to identify relevant terms and phrases buyers might use. Incorporate these keywords naturally into your titles, descriptions, and tags, aligning them with your product and buyer intent. Consider long-tail keywords catering to niche markets; they often have less competition and higher conversion rates. Continuously monitor and refine your SEO strategy, analyzing which keywords drive traffic and sales, adjusting your listings accordingly.

Setting Competitive Pricing Strategies

Establishing prices that are attractive to buyers while ensuring profitability is a delicate balance. Firstly, conduct thorough market research to understand pricing trends within your niche. Analyze similar products in terms of quality, materials used, and uniqueness to gauge their pricing.

Consider your production costs, including materials, labor, overheads, and your desired profit margin. Factor in any additional expenses like packaging or shipping supplies. While aiming for competitiveness, also reflect the value you offer—handmade craftsmanship, unique designs, or exceptional quality—that justifies a slightly higher price.

Moreover, periodic review and adjustment of your pricing strategy are crucial. Monitor sales trends, customer feedback, and changes in market dynamics. Be flexible to adapt your pricing based on seasonal demands, promotions, or evolving customer preferences. Offering occasional discounts, bundle deals, or loyalty programs can attract buyers and drive sales without compromising your bottom line.

Remember, transparent pricing instills trust in buyers. Clearly communicate your pricing rationale and the value they receive for their investment in your product. This transparency fosters a positive relationship and builds credibility, contributing to long-term success on Etsy.

Offering Shipping Options and Policies

Shipping plays a significant role in the overall customer experience. Begin by determining your shipping strategy—whether to offer free shipping, flat rates, or calculated rates based on location and weight. Free shipping can be an enticing offer but should be factored into your product pricing or used selectively for certain products.

Detail your shipping policies clearly and concisely in your shop's policies section. Address aspects such as processing times, handling, and estimated delivery. Be realistic about delivery times to manage buyer expectations and prevent dissatisfaction.

Consider Etsy's shipping tools and partnerships to streamline your shipping process. Use Etsy's integrated shipping labels or explore discounted rates with shipping carriers to reduce costs and simplify fulfillment. Offering tracking information for orders enhances transparency and provides reassurance to buyers.

To cover unforeseen circumstances, establish contingency plans for delays or shipping issues. Communicate promptly with buyers if any issues arise, offering solutions or alternatives to maintain a positive customer experience.

Lastly, consider packaging as part of the overall shipping experience. Invest in attractive and protective packaging that aligns with your brand's aesthetic. Thoughtful packaging can enhance the perceived value of your product and leave a lasting impression on buyers.

CHAPTER 3

Navigating Etsy's Tools

Utilizing Etsy's Seller Dashboard

The Seller Dashboard is your central hub for managing and tracking various aspects of your Etsy shop. It provides a comprehensive overview of your shop's performance, pending orders, important notifications, and key metrics. Upon accessing the Seller Dashboard, prioritize these functionalities:

Order Management: Keep track of new orders, pending shipments, and any unresolved customer inquiries or issues. Use the dashboard to process orders efficiently and provide timely updates to buyers.

Performance Overview: Monitor your shop's performance metrics, including sales trends, traffic sources, and conversion rates. Analyze this data to identify successful strategies and areas for improvement.

Notifications and Updates: Stay informed about important updates from Etsy, such as policy changes, promotions, or opportunities relevant to your shop. Respond promptly to any notifications requiring action.

Insights on Analytics and Shop Stats:

Etsy's Analytics and Shop Stats provide invaluable insights into your shop's performance, buyer behavior, and the effectiveness of your marketing efforts. Leverage these tools to make informed decisions and optimize your selling strategy:

Traffic and Conversion Data: Analyze the sources of traffic to your shop and which sources drive the most conversions. This helps tailor your marketing efforts towards the most effective channels.

Listing Performance: Assess which listings perform best in terms of views, favorites, and sales. Identify patterns in successful listings to replicate strategies for other products.

Customer Behavior: Understand customer demographics, preferences, and buying patterns. Use this information to adjust product offerings, pricing, or marketing strategies to better suit your target audience.

Seasonal Trends: Identify seasonal fluctuations in demand for your products. Plan ahead for peak seasons and adjust inventory, promotions, or marketing campaigns accordingly.

Promoted Listings and Advertising

Etsy's Promoted Listings and Advertising tools enable you to enhance your shop's visibility and reach a larger audience. These tools allow you to promote specific listings or your entire shop through paid advertising:

Promoted Listings: Identify high-performing products and create ad campaigns to increase their visibility within Etsy's search results and on-site placements. Set a budget and bid amount for each promoted listing, then monitor performance and adjust bids based on results.

Offsite Advertising: Utilize Etsy's offsite advertising feature to extend your reach beyond the Etsy platform. Etsy may feature your products on external platforms like Google, Facebook, or Instagram, charging a fee only when a sale is made through these ads.

Analyzing Ad Performance: Regularly review the performance of your promoted listings and offsite advertising campaigns through the Analytics dashboard. Evaluate metrics such as clicks, views, and return on ad spend (ROAS) to optimize your ad strategies.

CHAPTER 4

Providing Excellent Customer Service

Managing Orders and Fulfillment

Efficient order management and timely fulfillment are crucial components for a positive customer experience. Developing a structured workflow for order processing, including inventory management, packaging, and shipping, is essential. Set realistic processing times and communicate them clearly in your listings. Adhere rigorously to these timelines to meet or exceed customer expectations. Provide tracking information for orders to keep buyers informed about their shipment's progress, using Etsy's shipping tools or third-party services to streamline the process.

Handling Customer Inquiries and Communication

Responsive and informative communication is fundamental in fostering trust and satisfaction. Respond promptly to customer inquiries or messages, aiming for a response within 24 hours. Maintain a professional and friendly tone in all interactions, providing detailed and accurate information to address customer inquiries or custom requests. Proactively communicate potential issues or delays to buyers in advance, demonstrating commitment to customer satisfaction and transparency.

Resolving Disputes and Dealing with Feedback

Effectively resolving disputes and managing feedback can significantly impact shop reputation. Approach disputes with empathy and a problem-solving mindset, working with customers to find mutually beneficial solutions. Address negative feedback promptly and professionally, attempting to resolve the issue directly with the buyer before responding publicly. Utilize constructive criticism from feedback, both positive and negative, to improve your products and services.

Importance of Reviews and Building Reputation

Etsy reviews are integral to shaping your shop's reputation and attracting potential buyers. Positive reviews act as social proof and encourage trust among potential buyers. Encourage satisfied customers to leave reviews by providing exceptional service. Engage with reviews, expressing gratitude for positive feedback and addressing concerns in negative reviews professionally. Maintaining consistency in providing excellent service garners positive reviews consistently, building trust among buyers and leading to repeat purchases and referrals.

By focusing on efficient order management, clear communication, professional conflict resolution, and valuing customer feedback, you establish a reputation for excellent customer service on Etsy. Prioritizing customer satisfaction enhances credibility, attracts more buyers, and fosters long-term success in the competitive marketplace.

CHAPTER 5

Marketing and Growth Strategies

Social Media and Promotion

Leveraging Social Media for Etsy Marketing

Social media has emerged as a powerful tool for Etsy sellers to expand their reach, engage with audiences, and drive traffic to their shops. Here's a breakdown of effective strategies:

1. Choosing Platforms:

Identify social media platforms that align with your target audience. Platforms like Instagram, Pinterest, Facebook, and TikTok often work well for showcasing visually appealing products.

2. Compelling Visual Content:

Create high-quality visual content showcasing your products. Use engaging photos, videos, and graphics that highlight the uniqueness and craftsmanship of your items.

3. Consistent Branding:

Maintain a consistent brand aesthetic across social media platforms. Use similar colors, fonts, and messaging to reinforce brand identity and recognition.

4. Engaging Content Strategy:

Develop a content calendar with a mix of product posts, behind-the-scenes glimpses, customer testimonials, and relevant industry-related content.

Encourage interaction through polls, contests, and interactive stories to boost engagement and foster a sense of community.

5. Building a Community:

Interact authentically with your audience by responding to comments, messages, and user-generated content. Cultivate a relationship with your followers to build brand loyalty.

6. Utilizing Hashtags and SEO:

Use relevant and trending hashtags to increase the discoverability of your posts. Implement SEO techniques by including keywords in captions, titles, and descriptions.

7. Collaboration and Influencer Marketing:

Collaborate with influencers or micro-influencers whose audience aligns with your target market. Partnerships can amplify your reach and credibility.

8. Paid Advertising:

Consider investing in paid social media advertising to reach a wider audience. Platforms offer targeted ad options to reach specific demographics or interests.
Promotion Strategies for Etsy:

Promoting your Etsy shop beyond social media involves a mix of strategies to increase visibility and drive traffic:

1. Etsy Promoted Listings:

Utilize Etsy's Promoted Listings feature to boost the visibility of specific products within Etsy's search results. Set a budget and bid on relevant keywords.

2. Email Marketing:

Build an email list of customers and interested prospects. Send newsletters, exclusive offers, and updates about new products or promotions.

3. Collaborations and Partnerships:

Collaborate with other Etsy sellers, local businesses, or complementary brands for joint promotions, giveaways, or cross-promotions.

4. Discounts and Special Offers:

Offer limited-time discounts, coupons, or special deals to incentivize purchases and encourage repeat business.

5. Blogging and Content Marketing:

Start a blog related to your niche or products. Create valuable, informative content that educates, entertains, and drives traffic to your Etsy shop.

6. Offline Marketing and Events:

Participate in local markets, craft fairs, or trade shows to showcase your products. Hand out business cards or flyers with your Etsy shop details.

Scaling Your Etsy Business

Scaling an Etsy business involves a holistic approach, focusing on product development, operations, marketing, customer service, and long-term planning. Careful consideration of these facets and gradual implementation of strategies are key to successful and sustainable growth.

1. Product Diversification:
Scaling entails expanding your product range. List in-demand items within your niche, explore new variations, and introduce complementary products. Analyze market trends and customer preferences to guide your expansion strategy.

2. Streamlined Production:
Efficiency is crucial when scaling. Streamline production processes without compromising quality. Consider automation tools or outsourcing certain tasks to manage increased order volumes effectively.

3. Inventory Management:
Develop robust inventory management systems to handle a broader product line. Maintain optimal stock levels to meet demand without overstocking, minimizing storage costs.

4. Branding and Packaging:
Consistent branding across products fosters recognition. Invest in professional and appealing packaging to enhance the overall customer experience and reinforce brand identity.

5. Marketing and Promotion:
Diversify marketing efforts to reach a larger audience beyond Etsy. Invest in targeted advertising, collaborate with influencers, and optimize SEO strategies to expand visibility.

6. Customer Service Scalability:
Prepare for increased inquiries and orders by scaling customer service operations. Use templated responses for common queries and consider additional staffing if necessary.

7. Financial Management:
Meticulously manage finances as the business scales. Keep track of expenses, profits, and cash flow to ensure financial stability during expansion.

8. Outsourcing and Delegation:

Consider outsourcing or delegating tasks to free up time for strategic planning. Delegate responsibilities where possible to focus on growth initiatives.

9. Technology and Tools:

Invest in technology that aids scalability, such as inventory management software or analytics tools. Adopt systems that can handle increased demand and transactions.

10. Collaborations and Partnerships:

Leverage collaborations with other sellers, brands, or influencers to broaden your reach. Partnerships can amplify growth opportunities and access new markets.

11. Continuous Improvement:

Strive for continuous improvement. Regularly assess strategies, learn from mistakes, and adapt to changing market dynamics to stay competitive.

12. Scalable Systems and Infrastructure:

Build scalable systems and infrastructure to accommodate growth. Invest in platforms and processes capable of handling higher volumes efficiently.

13. Long-term Vision and Goals:

Define long-term goals aligned with a clear vision for the business. Ensure strategies are geared towards achieving these objectives while remaining adaptable to market changes.

14. Feedback and Adaptation:

Listen to customer feedback and adapt accordingly. Use this insight to refine products, services, and overall customer experience, ensuring alignment with customer needs and preferences.

QUIZ

This quiz is mainly to reinforce key concepts and knowledge introduced throughout the chapters. And to create an interactive and engaging experience, encouraging active participation and retention of essential information.

Question 1:

What is the primary purpose of creating an Etsy shop?
A) Connecting with friends
B) Selling handmade and vintage items
C) Sharing personal blogs
D) Joining an online community

Question 2:

What does SEO stand for in the context of Etsy selling?
A) Seller Engagement Opportunities
B) Search Engine Optimization
C) Selling Enhanced Offerings
D) Shop Efficiency Options

Question 3:

Which section of an Etsy listing is crucial for improving search visibility?
A) Item price
B) Shop location
C) Product description
D) Number of images

Question 4:

What is the maximum number of categories a product can be listed under in Etsy?
A) 1
B) 2
C) 3
D) 4

Question 5:

What is the primary purpose of Etsy's "Promoted Listings" feature?
A) Showcasing items in a virtual gallery
B) Boosting item visibility through paid ads
C) Offering free promotional items
D) Connecting sellers with influencers

Question 6:

What should be the primary focus when creating compelling product descriptions on Etsy?
A) Using complex language
B) Including irrelevant details
C) Highlighting product features and benefits
D) Omitting key information

Question 7:

Which factor greatly impacts the visibility of an Etsy shop in search results?
A) Shop's creation date
B) Number of product reviews
C) Seller's personal hobbies
D) Shop's logo design

Question 8:

What does "USP" stand for in the context of Etsy selling?
A) Unique Selling Proposition
B) Universal Selling Price
C) Updated Shop Preferences
D) User-Friendly Shop Pages

Question 9:

How can sellers gain insights into their shop's performance on Etsy?
A) By ignoring statistics
B) Through Etsy's Shop Manager
C) By avoiding customer feedback
D) By randomly changing product titles

Question 10:

Which section should sellers focus on to increase customer engagement in their Etsy shop?
A) Adding irrelevant tags
B) Enhancing product descriptions
C) Disabling customer reviews
D) Ignoring inquiries and messages